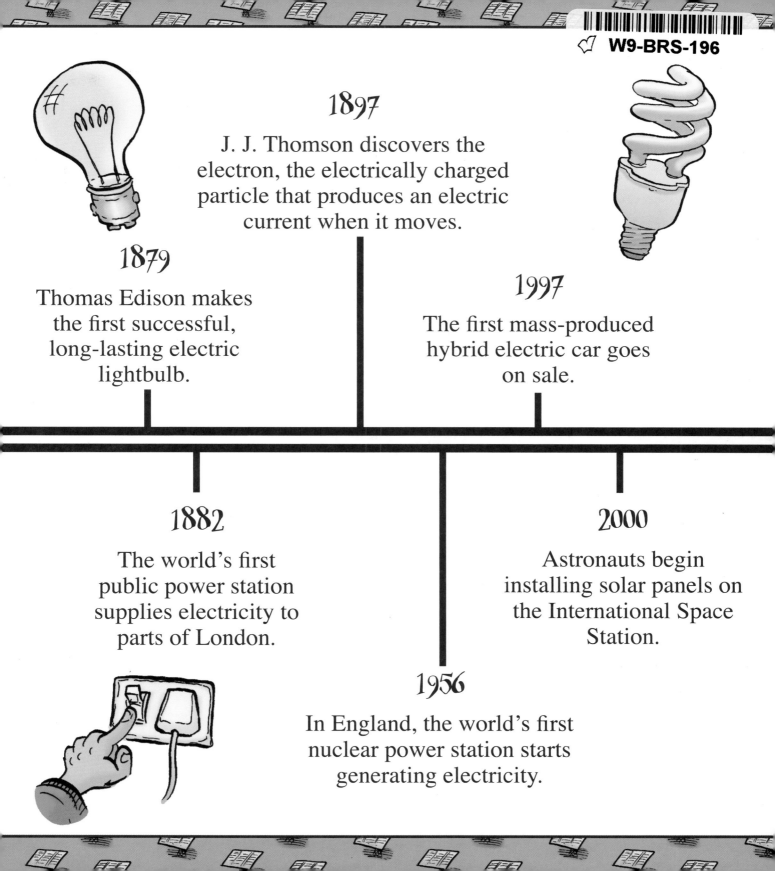

1897

J. J. Thomson discovers the electron, the electrically charged particle that produces an electric current when it moves.

1879

Thomas Edison makes the first successful, long-lasting electric lightbulb.

1997

The first mass-produced hybrid electric car goes on sale.

1882

The world's first public power station supplies electricity to parts of London.

2000

Astronauts begin installing solar panels on the International Space Station.

1956

In England, the world's first nuclear power station starts generating electricity.

Where Does Electricity Come From?

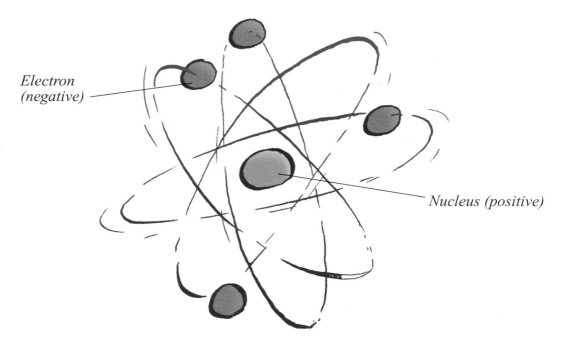

Electron
(negative)

Nucleus (positive)

Simple diagram of an atom

Electricity is produced by electric charges. And electric charges come from atoms. You and everything around you are made of atoms. The nucleus (middle) of an atom has a positive electric charge. Electrons flying around it are negatively charged. The positive and negative charges usually balance each other. But an atom can gain or lose electrons, and then the whole atom becomes electrically charged. This sort of electricity is called static electricity, because it stays in one place. But electrons can also jump from atom to atom. When electrons move in this way, they produce an electric current.

Author:

Ian Graham earned a degree in applied physics at City University, London. He then took a graduate diploma in journalism. Since becoming a freelance author and journalist, he has written more than 250 children's nonfiction books.

Artist:

Rory Walker is an artist and illustrator from deepest, darkest Snowdonia, Wales. He's created artwork for several hundred books and takes great delight in using a traditional pen and bottle of ink to create his images.

Series creator:

David Salariya was born in Dundee, Scotland. He has illustrated a wide range of books and has created and designed many new series for publishers in the UK and overseas. David established The Salariya Book Company in 1989. He lives in Brighton, England, with his wife, illustrator Shirley Willis, and their son, Jonathan.

Editors: **Caroline Coleman, Stephen Haynes**

Editorial Assistant: **Mark Williams**

© The Salariya Book Company Ltd MMXV
No part of this publication may be reproduced in whole or in part, or stored in a retrieval system, or transmitted in any form or by any means, electronic, mechanical, photocopying, recording, or otherwise, without written permission of the publisher. For information regarding permission, write to the copyright holder.

Published in Great Britain in 2015 by
The Salariya Book Company Ltd
25 Marlborough Place, Brighton BN1 1UB

ISBN-13: 978-0-531-21216-5 (lib. bdg.) 978-0-531-21307-0 (pbk.)

All rights reserved.
Published in 2015 in the United States
by Franklin Watts
An imprint of Scholastic Inc.
Published simultaneously in Canada.

A CIP catalog record for this book is available from the Library of Congress.

Printed and bound in China.
Printed on paper from sustainable sources.

1 2 3 4 5 6 7 8 9 10 R 24 23 22 21 20 19 18 17 16 15

SCHOLASTIC, FRANKLIN WATTS, and associated logos are trademarks and/or registered trademarks of Scholastic Inc.

PAPER FROM
SUSTAINABLE
FORESTS

You Wouldn't Want to Live Without™
Electricity!

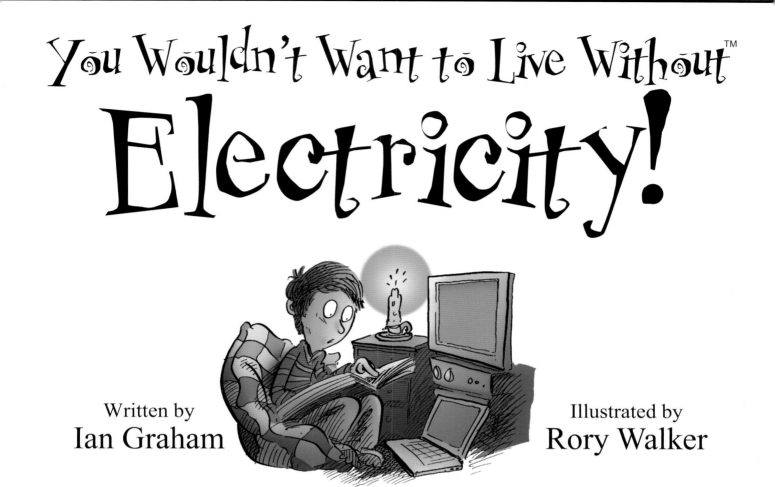

Written by
Ian Graham

Illustrated by
Rory Walker

Created and designed by
David Salariya

Franklin Watts®
An Imprint of Scholastic Inc.
NEW YORK • TORONTO • LONDON • AUCKLAND • SYDNEY
MEXICO CITY • NEW DELHI • HONG KONG
DANBURY, CONNECTICUT

Contents

Introduction

Electricity is invisible, but it's all around us in nature, and in our homes, schools, and workplaces. Electricity has existed for billions of years, but we have only been able to make it, control it, and use it for just over 200 years.

Nowadays, we can make electricity in all sorts of ways. We can make it from the energy in coal, oil, natural gas, the wind and waves, tides, sunlight, underground heat, atomic reactions, and even trash.

Billions of people all over the world rely on electricity. It makes modern life possible. Think of all the things you wouldn't be able to do if there were no electricity. Heating, lighting, communication, travel, transportation, and entertainment all depend on it. Without it, your life would be quite different. You wouldn't want to live without electricity!

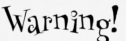

Warning!

ELECTRICITY CAN BE DANGEROUS!

- Don't touch electrical sockets and don't poke anything into them.

- Switch sockets off before pushing plugs in or pulling plugs out.

- Don't touch bare wires.

- Don't let electrical equipment get wet.

If the Lights Went Out

Many of the things we use in our everyday lives work because of electricity. What do you think life would be like if we had never discovered electricity, or if we suddenly had to do without it? Could you cope if the lights went out? What would you do if your television, computer, and phone stopped working? Just think—no social networks! How would you get around if there were no trains, buses, or cars? What would it be like without a refrigerator, freezer, washing machine, or vacuum cleaner? Without electricity, our lives would be colder, darker, duller, slower, and harder work.

IMAGINE WAKING up without electricity. You'll have to do without your bedside lamp and electric clock—don't oversleep! Your phone won't work either.

IF YOUR KITCHEN is all electric, you won't be having a hot breakfast, toast, or a hot drink. Sniff the milk for your cereal—without a fridge, it goes bad quickly.

DARK MORNINGS are even darker without streetlights. And you'll be walking to school, because cars, buses, and trains need electricity. The traffic lights are out. Your bike lights don't work either.

You Can Do It!

Make a list of all the things in your home that need electricity to work. Write down everything that plugs into a socket or needs batteries. You'll be surprised how many there are.

IS THERE WORK to be done around the house or garden? Without power tools, you'll have to rely on muscle power and hand tools.

IN THE EVENING you'll have to light a candle or two. Forget about watching TV, playing computer games, or going online. Thank goodness for books!

Light and Heat

30,000 YEARS AGO: The first lamps are hollowed-out stones filled with animal fat. A ball of moss or a plant stem soaks up the fat and burns. But these lamps aren't very bright.

We have had electric lights, heaters, and stoves in homes for the past 100 years. Before then, if you wanted light, heat, or a hot meal, you'd have to start a fire. The ancient Romans had central heating. It worked by sending hot air from a fire under a building's floor. Other people warmed their homes by burning wood or coal in open fires, but a lot of the heat escaped up the chimney. Homes were lit by candles or oil lamps, and later by gas lamps. All this burning was a terrible fire risk and it made towns very smoky.

2,000 YEARS AGO: Wealthy Romans have underfloor heating in their villas and bathhouses. It's called a hypocaust. Hot air from a fire is drawn through spaces under the floor and in the walls. Slaves keep the fire going.

Columns of brick beneath the floor

Hot air circulates between the columns

16th CENTURY: Candles have been used as lights for many hundreds of years. However, they give out very little light and they are blown out easily in drafty houses. They can start fires if they fall over. A candle lantern, like this one (left), is safer than a candle by itself.

17th CENTURY: Burning coal for heating is becoming popular. Coal burns hotter than wood and stays lit longer. However, coal is expensive, and coal fires produce a lot of smoke. Also, mining coal is a very dangerous job.

19th CENTURY: Kerosene lamps (left) are much brighter than candles. The wick is adjustable—winding it up produces a bigger flame—and the glass chimney protects the flame from drafts.

MID-19th CENTURY: Gas made from coal is piped into some homes. Coal-gas lamps (right) are bright, but the gas is dangerous. It can explode if it leaks, and it's also poisonous!

Tingles and Sparks

For thousands of years people live without electricity, but a few observant people begin to wonder about some strange effects in nature. When they stroke a cat, its fur sometimes stands on end and crackles. It may even make sparks.

When they rub a glassy material called amber, it picks up fine threads as if by magic. They don't know what causes these effects, because no one has figured that out yet. Our modern word "electricity," first used in the 17th century, comes from the ancient Greek word for amber—*elektron*.

ELECTRIC MEDICINE. The ancient Egyptians discovered that some catfish, rays, and eels can produce electric shocks. Ancient doctors are said to have used the high-voltage jolts from these fish to treat pain.

SCARY HAIR. Today we know that stroking a cat strips electrons off its fur, leaving the fur positively charged. The positive charges repel each other, so the strands of fur stand on end to get away from each other.

MAGIC AMBER. In ancient Greece, Thales of Miletus notices that when he rubs a piece of fossilized tree resin, called amber, small feathers stick to it. He has discovered what we now call static electricity, but he doesn't know it.

AROUND 300 BCE, the Greek teacher Theophrastus notices something very odd. When he heats a certain gemstone, small bits of dust, fluff, straw, and even pieces of wood move toward it. He probably used a gem that we know today as tourmaline. Heating some crystals, including tourmaline, produces static electricity. It's called pyroelectricity, from the Greek word for "fire," *pyr*.

11

Motors and Movement

100 BCE: The ancient Greeks and Romans use waterwheels to power machines. The waterwheels are often used to turn heavy grindstones to make flour. But if you don't have a handy river nearby, you can't use a waterwheel!

By medieval times, machines are driven by waterwheels, windmills, or muscle power. Then, in the eighteenth century, the steam engine is invented. Steam engines are a great improvement, because they don't depend on wind or on having a river nearby. Steam engines produce such fast growth in industry and railways that this time is called the Industrial Revolution. But the engines are big and heavy, and they need a constant supply of coal and water. They are eventually replaced by smaller gasoline and diesel engines. Later, electric motors are introduced. They are cleaner and easier to use.

600 CE: The Persians are probably the first people to use windmills for grinding grain. The early European mill shown here has sails covered with narrow strips of wood to catch the wind. Windmills work only when the wind blows.

1800s: Steam railroads are built to transport coal and iron, but they soon carry passengers, too. They make fast, long-distance travel possible for lots of people—but the smoke and soot are a nuisance for passengers.

1700s: The first steam engines are massive machines the size of a house. They burn coal to boil water and make steam. The steam turns a wheel that can drive machines such as water pumps. Steam engines produce lots of power, but they're smoky, noisy, and sometimes dangerous. Early ones have a habit of exploding!

You Can Do It!

Make a waterwheel. Cut four strips of stiff cardboard and attach them to an empty spool of thread. Push a long nail through the spool. Hold your waterwheel under running water so that the water hits the paddles on one side only.

It still takes muscle power to shovel the coal in, though!

Charging station

Modern electric car

LATE 19th CENTURY: The first electric cars are built in the 1880s, at about the same time as the first cars with gasoline engines. Some cars today are electric. They don't give out the harmful gases produced by other cars. Their batteries are charged by plugging them into a charging station.

13

Thunder and Lightning

In 1752, American scientist Benjamin Franklin watches flashes of lightning during thunderstorms and wonders if lightning might be a form of electricity. He carries out a very dangerous experiment to find out. He flies a kite near a thunderstorm. An iron key is tied to the end of the kite string. The kite string is attached to a metal wire running into a Leyden jar (see page 17), which will store the electric charge. Franklin holds on to the kite by a dry silk ribbon tied to the key, but when his hand moves too close to the key, he gets a shock. He is proved right: lightning is indeed electrical. Electricity from the clouds has traveled down the rain-soaked kite string to the key.

Warning!

NEVER COPY BENJAMIN FRANKLIN'S EXPERIMENT!

He was very lucky to survive—others who tried the same experiment were killed. Thunderclouds become charged with enormous amounts of electricity. A kite string gives the electric charge a path to the ground—right through the person holding the string!

Don't try this at home!

Kite string

Ribbon

Zing!

Iron key

Metal wire

Leyden jar

Lightning rod

Lightning conductor

Ground or earth rod

FRANKLIN REALIZES that lightning can be led safely down to the ground instead of damaging any buildings it strikes by attaching a metal rod from the roof down to the ground. When lightning strikes, the electricity travels harmlessly down the rod and into the ground. Franklin's invention is called the lightning rod. Today, all tall buildings have them.

IF YOU HEAR THUNDER, go indoors or get into a car. Close the car windows and don't touch anything metal. Never take shelter under trees or hold up an umbrella. If there is lightning and you can't get indoors, find the lowest spot possible, crouch down, and make yourself as small as you can.

You Can Do It!

Find out which items are conductors and which are insulators (see below) by making a tester. Connect two flashlight batteries (size D or smaller)* and a flashlight bulb with insulated copper wire. The bulb lights if the item you're testing is a conductor.

Batteries

Bulb

Test item

SOME MATERIALS let electric currents travel through them. They're called conductors. Other materials block electric currents. They're called insulators.

Which is which?

A CURRENT is a moving stream of electrons. Conductors have electrons that move easily from atom to atom. The electrons in an insulator are tightly held by their atoms and so electric currents cannot flow through them.

The Storage So Far

By the late 1700s, scientists and inventors have proved that electricity really exists. But unless they can catch it and store it, they can't study it. A dead frog comes to the rescue! Italian scientist Luigi Galvani is cutting one up when he sees its legs twitching as if it is receiving electric shocks. Another Italian scientist, Alessandro Volta, notices that the frog is hanging from a copper hook and that Galvani is using a steel knife. He wonders if the different metals have something to do with the twitching. This inspires Volta to build the first electric battery.

Galvani

I call it "animal electricity."

Have you tried a different hook?

Volta

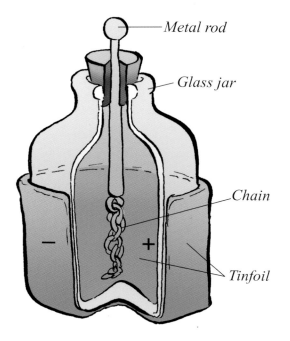

Metal rod

Glass jar

Chain

+

−

Tinfoil

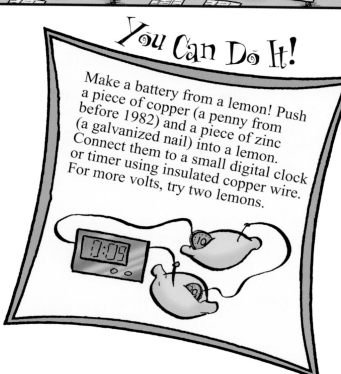

You Can Do It!

Make a battery from a lemon! Push a piece of copper (a penny from before 1982) and a piece of zinc (a galvanized nail) into a lemon. Connect them to a small digital clock or timer using insulated copper wire. For more volts, try two lemons.

1740s: THE LEYDEN JAR (above), a device for storing an electric charge, is invented by Ewald Georg von Kleist and Pieter van Musschenbroek. It's a glass jar coated with tinfoil inside and out. A metal rod is connected to the inside foil by a chain. Feeding electricity to the rod charges the inside foil.

1800: ALESSANDRO VOLTA makes the first battery. He makes it from a pile of copper and zinc plates with pads soaked in brine (salty water) or acid between each pair of plates.

TODAY: BE GRATEFUL that you don't have to use batteries like Volta's pile of dripping metal plates. Modern batteries produce more electricity—and the chemicals are sealed safely inside.

1780s: GALVANI (see page opposite) thinks the electricity is being made by the animal's muscles, like some sort of life force—but he is wrong. Volta realizes that the electricity is being created outside the animal in some way, and it then shocks the muscles into action.

Stack of metal plates

−

+

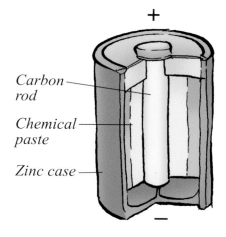

+

Carbon rod

Chemical paste

Zinc case

−

+ Positive terminal
− Negative terminal

Putting Electricity to Work

By the early 1800s, electricity can be generated and stored. Now, inventors start looking for new ways to use it. The next step involves a Dane, two Frenchmen, and an Englishman. Their work produces electric machines—motors and generators—that will change the world.

As usual, the first discovery is made by accident! In 1820, the Danish scientist Hans Christian Oersted is demonstrating an experiment to students at the University of Copenhagen when he notices something surprising and unexpected. It changes the way scientists think about electricity and magnetism, and leads to a series of important discoveries and inventions.

1820: HANS CHRISTIAN OERSTED is using an electric circuit to heat a wire when he notices that a compass needle nearby is moving. Every time the current from the battery is switched on or off, the magnetic needle jumps. Oersted has discovered that electricity and magnetism are linked.

1820s: ANDRÉ-MARIE AMPÈRE, a French scientist, learns of Oersted's discovery. He begins studying electricity and magnetism, and finally discovers the law of nature that links them—Ampère's Law. He has created a new branch of science: electromagnetism.

$$\nabla \times H = \frac{\partial}{\partial}$$

$$\oint H \cdot dL =$$

You Can Do It!

To make a simple motor, place a small, strong magnet* on the head of a steel screw. Dangle the screw from a 1.5-volt C-cell battery. Connect the other end of the battery to the side of the magnet with a wire and watch the screw start spinning.

*A neodymium button magnet works best.

Wire

Mercury

Magnet

Battery

1821: MICHAEL FARADAY invents the electric motor. A wire is dipped into a cup of mercury, a liquid metal. An electric current flows through the wire, making it spin around a magnet in the cup. It isn't very powerful, but it shows that an electric current can produce motion.

1832: HIPPOLYTE PIXII, a French instrument maker, invents the first practical electricity generator. Turning a handle spins a magnet close to two coils of wire. As the magnet turns, it makes an electric current flow through the wire coils.

Coils

Magnet

Power to the People

Transformer

THE LITTLE BOX you plug in to charge your phone is a transformer. It lowers the electricity supply to the smaller voltage needed to charge the phone. Transformers were invented in 1831 by Michael Faraday.

Now that useful amounts of electrical power can be generated, it's time to take electricity to the people. The world's first public power stations are built in Britain and the United States in the 1880s. Light and heat are finally available at the flick of a switch. But old habits are hard to break—the new lighting comes with a warning telling people not to light it with a match! At first, only the wealthiest people can afford to have their own electricity supply at home, but in the following years more homes are connected. The electric age has arrived!

It's astonishing, Father!

You Can Do It!

Electric current flows around a path called a circuit. To make a simple circuit, connect a battery* to a flashlight bulb with insulated copper wire. Electric current flows from the battery through the bulb and back to the battery, lighting the bulb.

Pylon

ELECTRICITY HAS TO BE MOVED from the power stations where it is generated to all the places where it is used. The current is sent along cables called transmission lines. The electricity is boosted to hundreds of thousands of volts, sent down the transmission lines, and then lowered to a safer voltage for homes. Transformers do the job of raising and lowering the voltage.

(1) *Power station generates electricity.*

(2) *Transformer boosts voltage.*

(3) *Transmission lines carry electricity over long distances.*

(4) *Transformer lowers voltage.*

(5) *Electricity is carried to homes on poles or underground.*

21

Sound and Vision

The first machines to play recorded sound and moving pictures are powered by clockwork motors or by turning a handle. Their sound quality is poor and their pictures are jerky. Electric recorders and players are a big improvement: their motors run at a steady speed. As radio and television come into fashion, electricity quickly becomes essential for everyday life. The computers, digital cameras, cell phones, DVD players, and MP3 players we use today would not exist without it.

SHOUTING THROUGH a big cone called a megaphone (left) is the only way to make your voice sound louder until the early 1900s, when electric amplifiers are invented.

1877: AMERICAN THOMAS EDISON invents the phonograph. It records sounds on cylinders (usually coated with wax) and plays them back. It is powered by turning a handle, not by electricity.

1888: EMILE BERLINER invents a rubber disk for recording sound. Later, disks were made of vinyl. The flat disks are simpler to make and easier to store than cylinders. This machine works by clockwork.

1888: THE FIRST POPULAR CAMERAS take photographs on plastic film sealed inside the camera. The camera has to be sent away so the film can be processed chemically.

REGULAR TELEVISION BROADCASTS begin in the 1930s, but not many people own a television set until the 1950s. At first the screens are small and the pictures are black and white.

It's as if they were in the same room as us!

Top Tip

To make a pinhole viewer: Cover one end of a cardboard tube with foil, held in place with a rubber band. Cover the other end with parchment paper. Make a hole in the foil with a needle. Point the foil end at something bright (NOT the Sun!) and look at the paper end. Can you see a picture?

Tablet computer

TODAY'S MOBILE DEVICES (right) are small, light, wireless, and powered by batteries, so you can take them anywhere.

Meanwhile, back at the ranch…

THE FIRST MOVIES have no sound. To make them more exciting, a pianist plays music to match the action on the screen. Captions explain the story.

THE FIRST RADIOS have electronic parts made of glass, called tubes or valves. They sometimes burn out or break and have to be replaced.

HOME ENTERTAINMENT TODAY is the result of more than a century of inventions in radio, television, photography, sound recording, and movies.

Fossil-Fuel Power

Most of the world's electricity is made from fossil fuels — mainly coal, oil, and natural gas. The energy locked up in these is released by burning the fuel. But there's a problem: when fossil fuels burn, they give out carbon dioxide. This gas soaks up heat from the Sun and holds on to it. The huge amounts of fossil fuels burned since the Industrial Revolution have produced so much carbon dioxide that the atmosphere is warming up. That's not good: a warmer atmosphere is a stormier atmosphere. And a warmer world has less ice and higher sea levels.

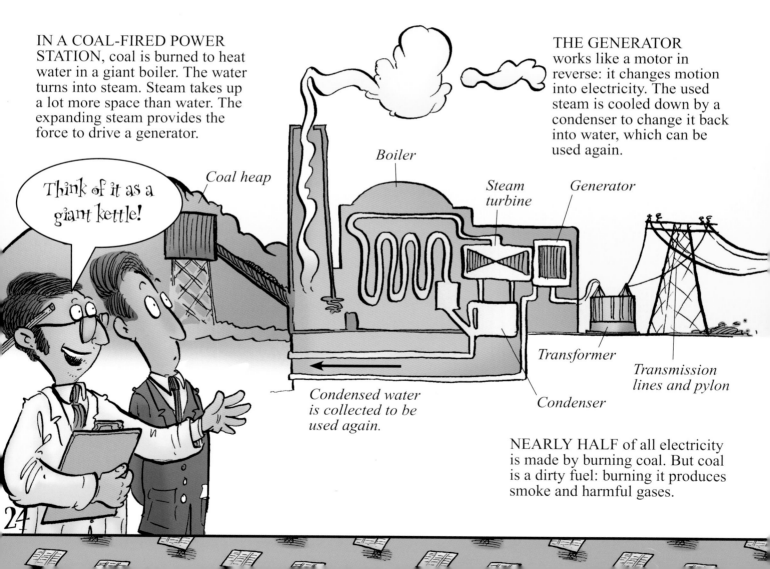

IN A COAL-FIRED POWER STATION, coal is burned to heat water in a giant boiler. The water turns into steam. Steam takes up a lot more space than water. The expanding steam provides the force to drive a generator.

THE GENERATOR works like a motor in reverse: it changes motion into electricity. The used steam is cooled down by a condenser to change it back into water, which can be used again.

Think of it as a giant kettle!

Coal heap

Boiler

Steam turbine

Generator

Transformer

Transmission lines and pylon

Condensed water is collected to be used again.

Condenser

NEARLY HALF of all electricity is made by burning coal. But coal is a dirty fuel: burning it produces smoke and harmful gases.

24

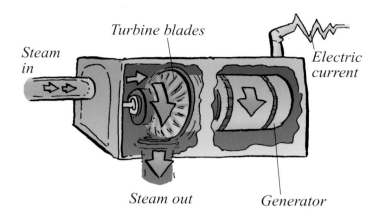

Steam in

Turbine blades

Electric current

Steam out

Generator

A TURBINE is a disk or drum with blades attached to it. When steam from a power station's boiler hits the blades, the turbine spins and turns the generator.

Top Tip

Green plants absorb carbon dioxide. If you plant a tree at home or at school, it will take a little carbon dioxide out of the atmosphere and help to reduce the warming effect of the gas on our planet. Plant your new young tree in spring and water it until it is strong.

Where Fossil Fuels Come From

FOSSIL FUELS were once plants and creatures that lived millions of years ago. When they died, they became buried under layers of soil and mud. Heat and pressure changed them into coal, oil, and gas.

COAL MINES produce nearly 9 billion tons (8 billion metric tons) of coal a year. Most of it is deep underground. Miners used to cut the coal by hand. Today, machines do the cutting, but mining work is still dangerous.

DRILLING RIGS on the land and in the sea bore down through the ground to reach oil and gas trapped deep under layers of rock. The weight of the rock pressing down sends the oil and gas shooting up to the surface.

Going Green?

If you don't want to use electricity made from fossil fuels, you have two options for cutting the amount of carbon dioxide produced. You could "go green" and use electricity made from cleaner natural sources, or you could rely on nuclear power stations. Natural energy sources include the wind, waves, tides, sunlight, underground heat, falling water, and even plants. All of these are called "renewables," because they are constantly renewed by nature. Nuclear electricity is generated by smashing atoms apart inside a nuclear reactor to produce heat. This heat is used to make electricity.

WIND TURBINES are modern windmills, but instead of grinding corn, they make electricity. Forests of wind turbines, called wind farms, are built in wild, windy places.

Green power is clean power!

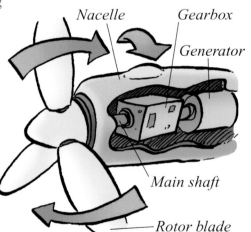

Nacelle

Gearbox

Generator

Main shaft

Rotor blade

THE BLADES of a wind turbine turn about 10 to 20 times a minute. The gearbox multiplies this to a higher speed of about 1,800 revolutions per minute to run the generator. The machinery is housed in a casing, or nacelle.

THE TIDES that wash up onto the land carry lots of energy. A tidal power generator guides the incoming and outgoing tides through a line of gates. Turbines in the gates spin as the water rushes through them.

GEOTHERMAL POWER STATIONS tap natural heat from deep underground. They pump water down more than 13,000 feet (4,000 meters). When it comes back to the surface, it's hot enough to make steam to power generators.

Top Tip

Power stations convert energy from one form into another. You convert energy, too. Riding a bike converts chemical energy in your muscles into kinetic energy, or energy of motion.

NUCLEAR POWER STATIONS smash atoms apart. When big atoms of uranium are broken up, they produce energy in the form of heat. This heat is then used to make steam.

HYDROELECTRIC POWER PLANTS (left) make electricity from falling or flowing water. A dam is built across a river to create a lake, or reservoir. Water flowing through the dam spins turbines that drive generators.

Solar panels

SUNLIGHT CARRIES ENERGY, called solar energy. Solar panels (right) are made of materials that change light directly into electricity. A different system uses the heat energy in sunlight to make steam.

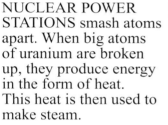

WAVE-POWER GENERATORS look like huge floating snakes. As waves rise and fall, the sections of the generator bend where they join. This bending motion is converted into electricity.

Save the Planet!

Many of the ways we make electricity today have drawbacks. Fossil fuels cause air pollution and they will run out one day—no more coal, oil, or natural gas! Wind turbines work only when the wind blows—no wind, no volts! Solar power stations work well only in bright sunshine. Nuclear power stations produce dangerous radioactive waste. Nuclear accidents can release lethal radiation. Scary!

You can help to reduce the bad effects of generating electricity by saving energy wherever possible so that less electricity has to be made.

EARTH DAY is held on April 22 every year to involve people in activities and campaigns that help the environment. It started in the United States in 1970 and has now spread around the world to about 200 countries.

Three Ways to Save Electricity

1. USE LESS ELECTRICITY. Switch things on only when you need them.

2. BE ENERGY-EFFICIENT. Use energy-saving lightbulbs and other devices.

3. RECYCLE. This reduces the amount of electricity needed to make new materials.

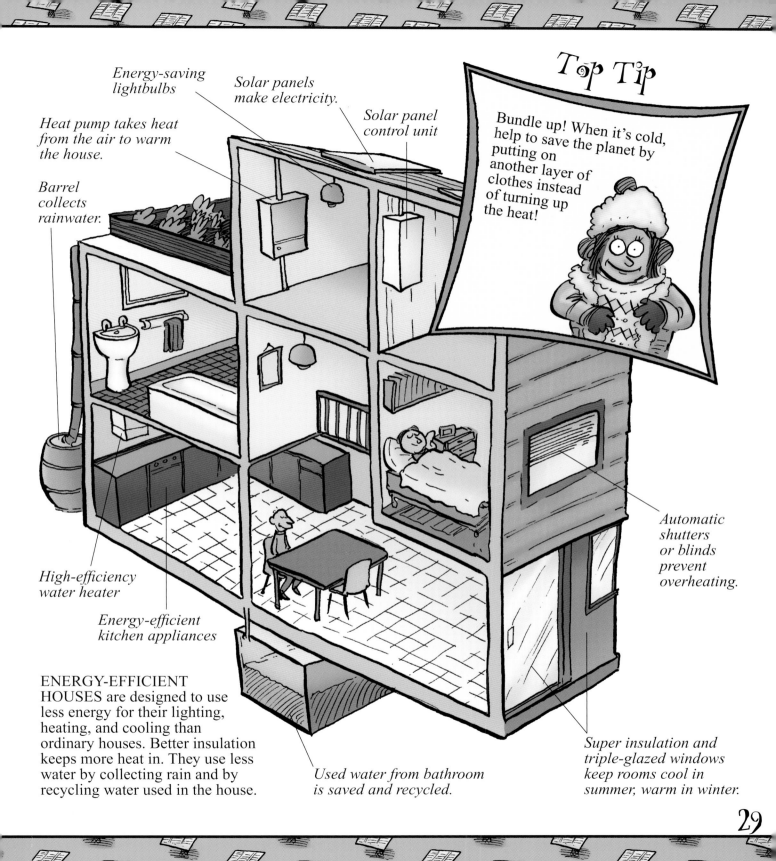

Energy-saving lightbulbs

Solar panels make electricity.

Solar panel control unit

Heat pump takes heat from the air to warm the house.

Barrel collects rainwater.

Top Tip

Bundle up! When it's cold, help to save the planet by putting on another layer of clothes instead of turning up the heat!

Automatic shutters or blinds prevent overheating.

High-efficiency water heater

Energy-efficient kitchen appliances

ENERGY-EFFICIENT HOUSES are designed to use less energy for their lighting, heating, and cooling than ordinary houses. Better insulation keeps more heat in. They use less water by collecting rain and by recycling water used in the house.

Used water from bathroom is saved and recycled.

Super insulation and triple-glazed windows keep rooms cool in summer, warm in winter.

Glossary

Air pollution Harmful gases and particles released into the air.

Amp A unit of electric current.

Atmosphere The gases that surround Earth or another planet, moon, or object in space.

Atoms The basic units of matter that solids, liquids, and gases are made of.

Battery A device that stores chemical energy and then converts it into electrical energy when connected to an electric circuit.

Boiler A vessel or tank in which water is heated to make steam.

Conductor A material that electricity and heat can flow through quickly.

Efficient Working in the best way, with the smallest amount of waste.

Electric circuit A path around which an electric current flows.

Electric current A flow of electrically charged particles.

Electric motor A machine that converts electricity into motion.

Electromagnetism The study of electric and magnetic forces and fields.

Electron A negatively charged particle. A flow of electrons forms an electric current.

Energy The ability to do work.

Environment The natural world.

Filament A thin wire that heats up and glows when a large electric current flows through it.

Fossil fuel A substance that formed from the buried remains of prehistoric plants and animals and is burned for heat or power. Coal formed from plants growing on land. Oil and gas formed from microscopic plants and creatures in the sea.

Gasoline A fuel made from oil.

Generator A machine that converts motion into an electric current.

Industrial Revolution The period from about 1760 to 1840 when many new forms of technology were developed, especially steam engines.

Insulator A material that is a poor conductor of electricity and heat.

Kerosene A fuel made from oil, used in household lamps.

Leyden jar An early device for storing an electric charge. One of its inventors was a university professor at Leyden (now spelled Leiden) in Holland.

Medieval Belonging to the Middle Ages, a period of history lasting roughly from the fifth century to the fifteenth.

Nucleus The center of an atom. It has a positive electric charge.

Particle A tiny piece of matter.

Recycle To use something again instead of throwing it away.

Renewables Sources of energy that are made again by nature, including sunlight, wind, tides, and waves.

Resists In electricity, when a material slows down an electric current as it passes through the material.

Solar panel A device that converts the energy in sunlight into electricity.

Static electricity A build-up of an electric charge.

Transformer A device for increasing or decreasing voltage.

Turbine A disk or drum with blades, like a multi-blade propeller, that spins when a liquid or gas flows through it.

Volt A unit of electric force—the force that pushes an electric current along.

Index

Top Discoverers of Electricity

Alessandro Volta (1745–1827)

The modern study of electricity began with Volta, an Italian physics professor. The electric battery that he invented was the first device that could supply a steady current of electricity. This enabled scientists to start experimenting with electricity and finding out more about it. The volt, the unit of electric force, is named after Volta. He also discovered the inflammable gas methane.

Michael Faraday (1791–1867)

This English scientist started his working life as an apprentice bookbinder. He read the books he worked on, which sparked an interest in science, especially electricity. He went on to discover electromagnetic induction (the principle behind the transformer), and he invented the electric motor. Faraday's discoveries enabled inventors to produce practical electrical devices and machines.

Beginning in 1825, Faraday gave a series of Christmas lectures about science for young people. These lectures still continue today at the Royal Institution in London. An electrical unit called the farad was named after him.

James Clerk Maxwell (1831–1879)

This Scottish scientist built on the work of pioneers such as Michael Faraday. He produced a set of equations that describes electricity, magnetism, and light as different forms of the same thing—electromagnetism. He also showed that electromagnetic waves travel through space at the speed of light. His work marked the beginning of modern physics. A unit of magnetism, the maxwell, was named after him.

The Future of Electricity

Today we are using more electricity than ever. As the world's population increases and more people use even more electricity, we will probably find all sorts of new ways to make it in the future.

Scientists have experimented with roads that generate electricity from the weight of heavy traffic moving along them. Buildings can be roofed with tiles that generate electricity from sunlight.

You might even wear shoes that generate electricity for your cell phone as you walk. And there may be a new type of power station that will produce heat for making electricity by nuclear fusion—the same process that powers the Sun.

Each time a new gadget is invented, there is even more demand for electricity.

1960s transistor radio

21st-century tablet computer